D1431323

On Love

Pierre Teilhard de Chardin

On Love

Harper & Row, Publishers

New York, Evanston, London,
San Francisco

Sur l'Amour
was first published in 1967 by
Editions du Seuil

© Editions du Seuil, 1967

© in the English translation of extracts from *The Evolution of Chastity*, William Collins Sons & Co. Ltd., London, 1972.

The other extracts reproduced here are taken from the following books: *The Phenomenon of Man* (© in the English translation William Collins Sons & Co. Ltd., London, and Harper & Brothers, New York, 1959); *Le Milieu Divin* (© in the English translation William Collins Sons & Co. Ltd., London, and Harper & Brothers, New York, 1960); *Writings in Time of War* (© in the English translation William Collins Sons & Co. Ltd., London, and Harper and Row, Publishers, Inc., New York, 1968); *Human Energy* (© in the English translation William Collins Sons & Co. Ltd., London, 1969). The original French editions of these books were published by Editions du Seuil, with the exception of *Writings in Time of War*, which was published by Editions Bernard Grasset.

FIRST U.S. EDITION

LIBRARY OF CONGRESS CATALOG CARD NUMBER: 72-86309

Contents

Extracts from

1 *Human Energy*, 'The Spirit of the Earth'   7

2 *Human Energy*, 'Sketch of a Personalistic Universe'   15

3 *The Evolution of Chastity*   27

4 *Writings in Time of War*, 'The Priest'   35

5 *Le Milieu Divin*, 'The Divine Milieu'   37

6 *Human Energy*, 'Human Energy'   41

7 *The Phenomenon of Man*, 'Beyond the Collective: the Hyper-Personal'   81

I

. . . Love is the most universal, the most tremendous and the most mysterious of the cosmic forces. After centuries of tentative effort, social institutions have externally dyked and canalized it. Taking advantage of this situation, the moralists have tried to submit it to rules. But in constructing their theories they have never got beyond the level of an elementary empiricism influenced by out-of-date conceptions of matter and the relics of old taboos. Socially, in science, business and public affairs, men pretend not to know it, though under the surface it is everywhere. Huge, ubiquitous and always unsubdued – this wild force seems to have defeated all hopes of understanding and governing it. It is therefore allowed to run everywhere beneath our civilization. We are conscious of it, but all we ask of it is to amuse us, or not to harm us. Is it truly possible for humanity to continue to live and grow without asking itself how much truth and energy it is losing by neglecting its incredible power of love?

From the standpoint of spiritual evolution, which we here assume, it seems that we can give a name and value to this strange energy of love.

Can we not say quite simply that in its essence it is the attraction exercised on each unit of consciousness by the centre of the universe in course of taking shape? It calls us to the great union, the realization of which is the only process at present taking place in nature. By this hypothesis, according to which (in agreement with the findings of psychological analysis) love is the primal and universal psychic energy, does not everything become clear around us, both for our minds and our actions? We may try to reconstruct the history of the world from outside by observing the play of atomic, molecular or cellular combinations in their various processes. We may attempt, still more efficaciously, this same task from within by following the progress made by conscious spontaneity and noting the successive stages achieved. The most telling and profound way of describing the evolution of the universe would undoubtedly be to trace the evolution of love.

In its most primitive forms, when life is scarcely individualized, love is hard to distinguish from molecular forces; one might think of it as a matter of chemisms or tactisms. Then little by little it becomes distinct, though still *confused* for a very long time with the simple function of reproduction. Not till hominization does it at last reveal the secret and manifold virtues of its violence.

'Hominized' love is distinct from all other love, because the 'spectrum' of its warm and penetrating light is marvellously enriched. No longer only a unique and periodic attraction directed to material fertility; but an unbounded and continuous possibility of contact through spirit much more than through body; the play of countless subtle antennae seeking one another in the light and darkness of the soul; the pull towards mutual sensibility and completion, in which preoccupation with preserving the species gradually dissolves in the greater intoxication of two people consummating a world. It is in reality the universe that is pressing on, through woman, towards man. The whole question (the vital question for the earth) is that they shall recognize one another.

If man fails to recognize the true nature, the true object of his love the confusion is vast and irremediable. Bent on assuaging a passion intended for the All on an object too small to satisfy it, he will strive to compensate a fundamental imbalance by materialism or an ever increasing multiplicity of experiments. His efforts will be fruitless – and in the eyes of one who can see the inestimable value of the 'spiritual quantum' of man, a terrible waste. But let us put aside any sentimental feelings or virtuous indignation. Let us look very coolly as biologists or engineers, at the lurid atmosphere of our great towns at evening. There, and everywhere else as well, the earth is continually dissipating its most marvellous power. This is pure loss. Earth is burning away, wasted on the empty air. How much energy do you think the spirit of the earth loses in a single night?

If only man would turn and see the reality of the universe shining in the spirit and through the flesh. He would then discover the reason for what has hitherto deceived and perverted his powers of love. Woman stands before him as the lure and symbol of the world. He cannot embrace her except by himself growing, in his turn, to a world scale. And because the world is always growing and always unfinished and always ahead of us, to achieve his love man is engaged in a limitless conquest of the universe and himself. In this sense, man can only attain woman by consummating a union with the universe. Love is a sacred reserve of energy; it is like the blood of spiritual evolution. This is the first revelation we receive from the sense of the earth.

– from *Human Energy*, translated by J. M. Cohen, pp. 32-4.

2

. . . The mutual attraction of the sexes is so fundamental that any explanation of the world (biological, philosophical or religious) that does not succeed in finding it a *structurally essential* place in its system is virtually condemned. To find such a place for sexuality in a cosmic system based on union is particularly easy. But this place must be clearly defined, both for the future and the past. What exactly are the essence and direction of 'passionate love' in a universe whose stuff is personality?

In its initial forms, and up to a very high stage in life, sexuality seems identified with propagation. Beings come together to prolong not themselves but what they have gained. So close is the link between pairing-off and reproduction that philosophers like Bergson have seen in it a proof that life has more existence than living beings; and religions as advanced as Christianity have hitherto based almost the whole of their moral code on the child.

But things look very different from the point of view to which the analysis of a structurally convergent cosmos has brought us. That the dominant function of sexuality was at first to assure the preservation of the species is indisputable. This was so until the *state* of personality was established in man. But from the critical moment of hominization, another more essential role was developed for love, a role of which we are seemingly only just beginning to feel the importance; I mean the necessary synthesis of the two principles, male and female, in the building of the human personality. No moralist or psychologist has ever doubted that these partners find a mutual completion in the play of their reproductive function. But hitherto this has been regarded only as a *secondary* effect, linked as an accessory to the principal phenomenon of reproduction. In obedience to the laws of the personal universe, the importance of these factors is tending, if I am not mistaken, to be reversed. Man and woman for the child, still and for so long as life on earth has not reached maturity. But man and woman for one another increasingly and for ever.

In order to establish the truth of this picture, I cannot do otherwise or better than resort to the sole criterion that has guided our progress throughout this study: that is to say bring the theory into the most perfect possible coherence with a vaster realm of reality. If man and woman were, I will say, principally for the child, then the role and power of love would diminish as human individuality is achieved, and the density of population on the earth is reaching saturation point. But if man and woman are principally for one another, then we imagine that with the growth of humanization they will feel an increasing need to draw closer. Now our experience proves that this is the actual state of things and that the other is not. It must therefore be explained.

In the hypothesis here accepted of a universe in process of personalization, the fact that love is increasing instead of diminishing in the course of hominization has a very natural explanation, and extension into the future. In the human individual, as we have already said, evolution does not close on itself, but continues further towards a more perfect concentration, linked with further differentiation, also obtained by union. Woman is for man, we should say, precisely the end that is capable of releasing this forward movement. Through woman and woman alone, man can escape from the isolation in which, even if perfected, he would still be in danger of being enclosed. Hence it is no longer strictly correct to say that the mesh of the universe is, in our experience, the thinking monad. The complete human molecule is already around us: a more synthesized element and more spiritualized from the start, than the individual personality. It is a duality, comprising masculine and feminine together.

Here the cosmic role of sexuality appears in its full breadth. And here at the same time, the rules appear which will guide us in the mastery of that terrifying energy, in which the power that causes the universe to converge on itself passes through us.

The first of these rules is that love, in conformity with the general laws of creative union, contributes to the spiritual differentiations of the two beings which it brings together. The one must not absorb the other nor, still less, should the two lose themselves in the enjoyments of physical possession, which would signify a lapse into plurality and return to nothingness. This is current experience, but can only be properly understood in the context of spirit-matter. Love is an adventure and a conquest. It survives and develops

like the universe itself only by per-
petual discovery. The only right
love is that between couples whose
passion leads them both, one
through the other, to a higher
possession of their being. The gravity
of offences against love therefore is
not that they outrage some sort of
modesty or virtue. It is that they
fritter away, by neglect or lust, the
universe's reserves of personalization. This wastage is the true explanation of the disorders of 'impurity'.
And at a higher degree in the de-
velopment of union this same wastage occurs in a subtler form, chang-
ing love into a joint egoism.

. . . When two beings between
whom a great love is possible manage
to meet among a swarm of other

beings, they tend immediately to enclose themselves in the jealous possession of their mutual gain. Impelled by the fulfilment that has engulfed them, they try instinctively to shut themselves into one another, to the exclusion of the rest. And even if they succeed in overcoming the voluptuous temptations of absorption and repose, they attempt to reserve the promises of the future for their mutual discovery, as if they constituted a *two-person universe*.

Now after all that we have said about the probable structure of the spirit, it is clear that this dream is only a dangerous illusion. In virtue of the same principle that compelled 'simple' personal elements to complete themselves in the pair, the pair in its turn must pursue the achievements that its growth requires beyond itself. And in two ways. On the one hand it must look outside itself for groupings of the same order with which to associate with a view to centring itself further ... On the other hand, the centre towards which the two lovers converge by uniting must manifest its personality at the very heart of the circle in which their union wishes to isolate itself. Without coming out of itself, the pair will find its equilibrium only in a third being ahead of it. What name must we give to this mysterious 'intruder'?

For so long as the sexualized elements of the world had not reached the stage of personality, progeny alone could represent the reality in which the authors of generation in some way prolonged themselves. But as soon as love came into play, no longer only between parents but between two persons, the final goal necessarily appeared more or less indistinctly ahead of the lovers, the place at which not only their race but their personality would be at once preserved and completed. Then the 'fall forward', of which we have already followed the adventures, begins once more. Stage by stage it must go on till the end of the world. And finally it is the total centre itself, much more than the child, that appears necessary for the consolidation of love. Love is a three term function: man, woman and

God. Its whole perfection and success
are bound up with the harmonious
balance of these three elements.

- from *Human Energy*, translated by
  J. M. Cohen, pp. 72-6.

3

. . . A real nobility of passion lends wings; and that is why the best test for gauging the sublimity of a love would be to note how decisively it develops in the direction of a greater freedom of spirit. The more spiritual the affection, the less it sucks up into itself – and the stronger its impulse towards action.

. . . love stands as the threshold of another universe. Beyond the vibrations that are familiar to us, the rainbow of its merging colours is con-

27

stantly and vigorously extending; but, for all the charm of the tints in the lower ranges, it is only in the direction of the 'ultra' that the creation of light makes real progress. It is in those invisible – we might almost say immaterial – areas that we can look for true initiation into unity. *The depths we attribute to matter are no more than the reflection from the heights of spirit.*

All human experience and thought, I believe, show that this is undeniable.

... I have come to the point where, it seems to me, two phases in the creative transformation of human love are emerging for me. During a first phase of humanity, man and woman concentrate upon the physical act of giving and the concern for reproduction: at the same time a growing nimbus of spiritual exchanges is gradually being built up around this fundamental act. At first this nimbus was no more than an imperceptible fringe; slowly, and yet ever more clearly, there is a shift, and the fruitfulness and mystery of union move into that zone: and it is on that side that the balance finally gives way and comes to rest. At that very moment, however, the centre of physical union from which the light was radiating is found to be incapable of accepting any further intensification. The focus of attraction suddenly shifts further and further – endlessly, indeed – ahead. If the lovers are to be able to continue to increase their mutual possession in spirit, they have to turn away from the body and look for one another in God. Virginity rests upon chastity as thought rests upon life: each is arrived at through a reversal of direction, or by passing through one unique point.

Such a transformation, of course, cannot be effected instantaneously on the surface of the earth: time is essential. When you heat water, the whole volume does not turn into steam at once – the 'liquid phase' and the 'gaseous phase' are found together for some time, and this must necessarily be so. Nevertheless, that duality covers but one single developing event – the direction and 'dignity' of which are shared by the whole. Thus, at the present moment, physical union still retains its value and necessity for the human race; but its spiritual quality is now defined by the higher type of union to which it has served as the preliminary and which it now fosters. Within the noosphere, love is now undergoing a 'change of state'; and it is in this new direction that mankind's collective entry into God is being organized.

This is how I see the evolution of chastity.

There is no theoretical difficulty about this transformation of love. All that is needed to effect it is that the appeal of the *personal* divine centre be felt with such intensity that it overcomes the natural attraction whose pull would tend prematurely to fling together the pairs of human monads.

From the practical point of view, however, I must confess that the suggestion presents such difficulty that what I have written here would be dismissed by nine people out of ten as over-ingenuous or even wildly extravagant. Does not universal experience show conclusively that spiritual loves have always come to a sordid end? Man is made to keep his feet firmly on the ground – flight has always been beyond our dreams. . . .

I am quite sure about my answer; yes, there have been madmen with such a dream, and that is why we have now conquered the air. What paralyses life is lack of faith and lack of courage. The difficulty lies not in solving problems but in expressing them correctly; and we can now see that it is biologically undeniable that unless we harness passion to the service of spirit there can be no progress. Sooner or later, then, and in spite of all our incredulity, the world will take this step – because the greater truth always prevails and the greater good emerges in the end.

The day will come when, after mastering the ether, the winds, the tides, gravity, we shall master the energies of love, for God. And then, for the second time in the history of the world, man will have made fire his servant.

– from *The Evolution of Chastity* (un-published), translated by René Hague.

4

And this means but one thing, Lord; that through the whole width and breadth of the Real, through all its past and through all that it will become, through all that I undergo and all that I do, through all that I am bound by, through every enterprise, through my whole life's work, I can make my way to you, be one with you, and progress endlessly in that union.

With a fullness no man has conceived you realized, through your incarnation, love's threefold dream: to be so enveloped in the object of love as to be absorbed in it – endlessly to intensify its presence – and, without ever knowing surfeit, to be lost in it.

I pray that Christ's influence, spiritually substantial, physically mortifying, may ever spread wider among all beings, and that thence it may pour down upon me and bring me life.

I pray that this brief and limited contact with the sacramental species may introduce me to a universal and eternal communion with Christ, with his omni-operant will and his boundless mystical body.

– from *Writings in Time of War*, translated by René Hague, pp. 217-18.

5

What I cry out for, like every being, with my whole life and all my earthly passion, is something very different from an equal to cherish: it is a God to adore.

To adore . . . That means to lose oneself in the unfathomable, to plunge into the inexhaustible, to find peace in the incorruptible, to be absorbed in defined immensity, to offer oneself to the fire and the transparency, to annihilate oneself in proportion as one becomes more deliberately conscious of oneself, and to give of one's deepest to that whose depth has no end. Whom, then, can we adore?

The more man becomes man, the more will he become prey to a need, a need that is always more explicit, more subtle and more magnificent, the need to adore.

Disperse, O Jesus, the clouds with your lightning! Show yourself to us as the Mighty, the Radiant, the Risen! Come to us once again as the Pantocrator who filled the solitude of the cupolas in the ancient basilicas! Nothing less than this Parousia is needed to counter-balance and dominate in our hearts the glory of the world that is coming into view. And so that we should triumph over the

world with you, come to us clothed
in the glory of the world.

– from *Le Milieu Divin*, translated by
Bernard Wall, pp. 117-18.

6

. . . For the last century, without greatly noticing it, we have been undergoing a remarkable transformation in the range of intellect. To discover and know has always been a deep tendency of our nature. Can we not recognize it already in cave man? But it is only yesterday that this essential need to know has become explicit and changed into a vital autonomous function, taking precedence in our lives over our preoccupation with food and drink.

Now, if I am not mistaken, this phenomenon of the individualization of our highest psychological functions is not only far from having reached its limits in the field of pure thought, but is also tending to develop in a neighbouring realm, which has remained practically undefined and unexplored: the '*terra ignota*' of the affections and love.

Paradoxically, love (I understand love here in the strict sense of 'passion'), despite (or perhaps precisely because of) its ubiquity and violence, has hitherto been excluded from any rational systematization of the energy of man. Empirically, morality has succeeded more or less successfully in codifying its practice with a view to the maintenance and material propagation of the race. But has anyone seriously thought that beneath this turbulent power (which is nevertheless well known to be the inspirer of genius, the arts and all poetry) a formidable creative urge has remained in reserve, and that man will only be truly man from the day when he has not only checked, but transformed, utilized and liberated it? Today, for our century, avid to lose no energy and to control the most intimate psychological mechanism, light seems to be beginning to break. Love, like thought, is still in full growth in the noosphere. The excess of its growing energies over the daily diminishing needs of human propagation becomes every day more manifest. And love is therefore tending in a purely hominized form, to fill a much larger function than the simple urge to reproduction. Between man and woman a specific and mutual power of spiritual sensitization and fertilization is probably still slumbering. It demands to be released, so that it may flow irresistibly towards the true and beautiful. Its awakening is certain. Expansion, I have said, of an ancient power. The expression is undoubtedly too weak. Beyond a certain degree of sublimation spiritualized love, by the boundless possibilities of intuition and communication it contains, penetrates the unknown; it will in our sight take its place, in the mysterious future, with the group of new faculties and consciousnesses that is awaiting us.

. . . Union, the true upward union in the spirit, ends by establishing the elements it dominates in their own perfection. *Union differentiates.* In virtue of this fundamental principle, elementary personalities can, and can *only* affirm themselves by acceding to a psychic unity or higher soul. But this always on one condition: that the higher centre to which they come to join *without mingling together* has its own autonomous reality. *Since there is no fusion or dissolution* of the elementary personalities the centre in which they join *must necessarily be distinct from them, that is to say have its own personality.*

Hence we have the following

formula for the supreme goal towards which human energy is tending: an organic plurality the elements of which find the consummation of their own personality in a paroxysm of mutual union and limpidity: the whole body being supported by the unifying influence of a *distinct centre* of super-personalization.

This last condition or qualification has considerable importance. It demonstrates that the noosphere in fact *physically* requires, for its maintenance and functioning, the existence in the universe of a true pole of psychic convergence: a centre different from all the other centres which it 'super-centres' by assimilation: a personality distinct from all the personalities it perfects by uniting with them. The world would not function if there did not exist, somewhere ahead in time and space, 'a cosmic point Omega' of total synthesis.

Consideration of this Omega will allow us to define more completely in a concluding chapter, the hidden nature of what we have till now called vaguely enough, 'human energy'.

LOVE, A HIGHER FORM OF HUMAN ENERGY

. . . In us and around us, we have been able to conclude, the world's units are continually and increasingly personalizing, by approaching a goal of unification, itself personal; in such a way that the world's essential energy definitely radiates from this goal and finally flows back towards it; having confusedly set the cosmic mass in motion, it emerges from it to form the noosphere.

What name should we give to an influence of this sort?

Only one is possible: love.

Love is by definition the word we use for attractions of a personal nature. Since once the universe has become a thinking one everything in the last resort moves in and towards personality, it is necessarily love, a kind of love, which forms and will increasingly form, in its pure state, the material of human energy.

Is it possible to verify *a posteriori* this conclusion which is imposed on us *a priori* by the conditions of functioning and maintenance of the thinking activity of the earth's surface?

Yes, I believe so. And in two different ways.

Psychologically, first, by observing that love carried to a certain degree of universality by a perception of the centre Omega is the only power capable of totalizing the possibilities of human action without internal contradictions.

Then *historically*, by observing that such a universal love actually presents itself to our experience as the highest term of a transformation already begun in the mass of the noosphere.

Let us try to demonstrate this.

1. Love, the Totalizing Principle of Human Energy

Those who greet with the greatest scepticism any suggestion tending to promote a general co-ordination of thought on earth are precisely the first to recognize and deplore the state of division in which human energies are vegetating: disconnected actions by the individual, disconnected individuals in society. It is evident, they say, that a vast power is neutralized and lost in this unordered movement. But how can you expect dust like this to cohere? Themselves already divided by nature, these human particles continue to repel one another irremediably. You might perhaps force them mechanically together. But to infuse a common soul into them is a physical impossibility.

The strength and weakness of all these objections to the possibility of some eventual unification of the world seem to depend on the fact that they insidiously exaggerate appearances which are only too real, without being willing to take into account certain new factors already perceptible in humanity. The pluralists always reason as if no principle of connexion existed, or tended to exist, in nature outside the vague or superficial relations habitually examined by common sense and sociology. They are at bottom juridicists and fixists who cannot imagine anything around them except what seems to them always to have been there.

But let us see what will happen in our souls the instant there emerges, at the moment fixed by the march of evolution, the perception of an animated universal centre of convergence. Let us imagine (this is no fiction, as we shall soon state) a man who has become conscious of his personal relations with a supreme personality, to whom he is led to add himself by the entire play of cosmic activities. In such a man, and starting with him, a process of unification has inevitably begun, which will be divided into the following stages: totalization of each operation in regard to the individual; totalization of the individual in regard to himself; and finally, totalization of individuals in collective humanity. All this 'impossibility' taking place naturally under the influence of love.

a. Totalization by Love of Individual Actions

In the divided state in which the pluralists consider us (that is to say outside the conscious influence of Omega) we most often act only from a tiny portion of ourselves. Whether eating or working, or doing mathematics or a crossword puzzle, man is only partially engaged in his activity, with only one or another of his faculties. His senses, or his limbs, or his reason function, but never his heart itself. Human action but not the action of a whole man, as a scholastic would say. That is why after a life of highest effort, a scientist or thinker may end up impoverished and desiccated – disillusioned; his mind but not his personality has worked on inanimate objects. He has given himself; he has not been able to love.

Let us now observe the same forms of activity in the light of Omega. Omega, in which all things converge, is reciprocally that from which all things radiate. Impossible to place it as a point at the peak of the universe without at the same time diffusing its presence within each smallest advance of evolution. The meaning of this is nothing less than this: that *for him who has seen it* everything, however humble, *provided it places itself in the line of progress*, is warmed, illumined and animated, and consequently becomes an object to which he gives his *whole* adhesion. What was cold, dead, impersonal for him who cannot see, becomes charged for those who see not only with life but with a stronger life than theirs; in such a way that they feel themselves seized and assimilated, as they act, to a far greater degree than they themselves are seizing and assimilating. Where the former only finds an object with limited reactions, the latter are able to expand with the totality of their powers – to love the lowest of their tasks as passionately as if they could touch or caress it. In the external appearance of the operation there is no change. But what a difference in the stuff of the action, in the intensity of the gift! The whole distance between consumption and communion.

And this is the first step in totalization. Within a world of personal and convergent structure, in which attraction becomes love, man discovers that he can give himself boundlessly to everything he does. In the least of his acts he can make an entire contact with the universe, with the whole surface and depth of his being. Everything has become a complete nourishment to him.

b. *Totalization of the Individual on Himself by Love*

That each of our separate pursuits can become *total* under the animating influence of Omega is already a marvellous utilization of human energy. But no sooner has this first transfiguration of our activities taken shape than it tends to enlarge into another more profound metamorphosis. By the very fact that they become total, each one in itself, our activities are logically led to totalize, merged together in a single act. Let us see how.

The immediate effect of universal love, rendered possible by Omega, is to attach to each of our actions a root identity of passionate involvement and gift of self. What will the influence of this common ground (one might call it this new climate) be on our inner life? Shall we dissolve under its pleasant warmth? Will it blur the clear outline of the objects around us with an atmosphere of mirage? Will it take our attention from the individual and tangible, to absorb us in a confused sense of the universal? If we fear this, it is because we have again forgotten that in the direction of spirit union differentiates. It is undoubtedly true that once I have discovered Omega, all things become for me in some ways the same thing; so that whatever I do I shall have the impression of doing one and the same thing. But this fundamental unity has nothing in common with a melting into homogeneity. In the first place, far from weakening, it accentuates the outline of the elements it assembles; for Omega, the sole object of desire, only forms for our eyes and offers itself to our touch in the completion of those elementary advances by which the fabric of evolution is empirically taking shape. But there is more to it than this. Love not only impregnates the universe like an oil that will revive its colours. It does not simply bind the clouded dust of our experiences into a common lucidity. It is a true *synthesis* which operates on the grouped bundle of our faculties. And this is indeed the point which it is most important to understand.

In the superficial course of our existences, there is a difference between seeing and thinking, between understanding and loving, between giving and receiving, between growing and shrinking, between living and dying. But what will happen to all those contradictions once their diversity has revealed itself in Omega as an infinite variety of forms of a single universal contact? Without any sort of radical disappearance they will tend to combine into a common sum, in which their still recognizable plurality will burst forth in ineffable riches. Not any sort of interference, but a resonance. Why should we be surprised? Do we not know, at a lesser degree of intensity, a similar phenomenon in our own experience? When a man loves a woman with a strong and noble passion that exalts his being above its common level, that man's life, his powers of feeling and creation, his whole universe, are definitely held and at the same time sublimated by his love of that woman. But however necessary the woman may be to that man, to reflect, reveal, transmit and 'personalize' the world for him, she is still not the centre of the world! If therefore the love of one unit for another is powerful enough to melt (without fusing) the multitude of our perceptions and emotions into a single impression, how great must be the vibration drawn from our beings by their encounter with Omega?

Indeed we are called by the music of the universe to reply, each with his own pure and incommunicable harmonic. When, as love for the All advances in our hearts, we feel stretching out beyond the diversity of our efforts and desires the bounding simplicity of an urge in which the innumerable shades of passion and action mingle in exaltation without ever becoming confused, then, within the mass formed by human energy, we shall each approach the plenitude of our powers and personality.

c. *Totalization by Love of Individuals in Humanity*

The transition from the individual to the collective is the present crucial problem confronting human energy. And it must be recognized that the first steps towards its solution only increase our consciousness of its difficulties. On the one side the ever tighter network of economic links, together with an indubitable biological determinism, inevitably presses us against one another. On the other, in the course of this compression, we seem to feel the most precious part of ourselves – our spontaneity and liberty – perishing. Totalitarianism and personalism: contrary to our theoretical expectations, must these two functions necessarily vary in inverse proportion to one another? In order to build the future (for we must certainly go forward) have we to choose between the Charybdis of collectivism and the Scylla of anarchy, between a mechanizing symbiosis and a devitalizing dispersion, between a termite colony and the Brownian movement? This dilemma, long evident to the clear-sighted, seems now suddenly to be entering the field of public notice. For the last year there has been no review or conference in which the question has not been broached. But the outline of a good solution has, alas, never been put forward.

The reason, in my opinion, for the disturbing checks suffered by humanity during the last century in its efforts to organize itself is not to be attributed to some natural obstacle inherent in the undertaking itself, but to the fact that the attempts at grouping are made by inverting the natural order of factors of the projected union. Let me explain.

To totalize without depersonalizing. To save the assemblage and the units at the same time. Everyone agrees that this is the dual task to be accomplished. But how do present-day social groups (democrats, communists, fascists) rate the values they theoretically agree in wishing to preserve? They all consider the individual as secondary and transitory, and place the primacy of the pure totality at the head of their programmes. In all the systems of human organization battling before our eyes, it is assumed that the final state towards which the noosphere is tending is a body without an individualized soul, a faceless organism, a diffuse humanity, an *Impersonality*!

Now once this point of departure is accepted, it vitiates the whole subsequent progress of the operation, to the extent of making it impractical. In a synthesizing process, the character finally impressed on the unified elements is necessarily that which permeates the active unifying principle. The crystal gives geometrical form to, the cell animates the matter that joins it. If the universe is tending finally to become *something*, how can it keep a place in itself for *Someone*? If the peak of human evolution is regarded as impersonal by nature, the units accepting it will inevitably, in spite of all efforts to the contrary, see their personality diminishing under its influence. And this is exactly what is happening. The servants of material progress or of racial entities may try their hardest to emerge into freedom, but they are fatally sucked in and assimilated by the determinisms they construct. Their own machinery turns them into machines. The true Hindu karma. And at this moment all that remains to control the machinery of human energy is the use of brute force – the same force that is very logically being offered us at present as an object of worship.

Now this is treason against spirit, and at the same time a grave mistake in human technology. A system formed of elements of consciousness can only cohere on a basis of immanence. Not force but love above us; and therefore, *at the beginning*, the recognized existence of an Omega that makes possible a universal love.

The mistake, as we have said, of modern social doctrines is to present enthusiasts for human effort with an *impersonal* humanity. What would happen on the day we recognized, instead of this blind divinity, the presence of a conscious centre of total convergence? Then by the opposite determinism to the one against which we are struggling, individualities, caught in the irresistible current of human totalization, would feel themselves strengthened by the very movement that brings them together. The more they grouped themselves under a personality, the more forcibly they would themselves become personal. And quite naturally, without effort, by virtue of the properties of love.

We have already several times stressed the capital truth that 'union differentiates'. Love is only the concrete expression of this metaphysical principle. Let us imagine an earth on which human beings were primarily (and even in a sense exclusively) concerned with achieving global accession to a passionately desired universal being, whom each one would recognize as a living presence in the most incommunicable features of his neighbour. In such a world, constraint would become useless as a means of keeping individuals in the most favourable condition for action, of guiding them in free competition towards better social groupings, of making them accept the restrictions and sacrifices imposed by a certain human selection, of deciding them once and for all not to waste their power of love but to raise it carefully and husband it for the final union. Under these conditions life would finally escape (supreme liberation) from the tyranny of material coercions; and a personality of increasing freedom would grow up without opposition within the totality.

'Love one another.' Those words were pronounced two thousand years ago. But today they sound again in our ears in a very different tone. For centuries charity and fraternity could only be presented as a code of moral perfection, or perhaps as a practical method of diminishing the pains or frictions of earthly life. Now since the existence of the noosphere, on the one hand, and the vital necessity we are under of preserving it, on the other, have been revealed to our minds, the voice which speaks takes on a more imperious tone. It no longer says only: 'Love one another in order to be perfect,' but adds, 'Love one another or you perish.' 'Realistic' minds are welcome to smile at dreamers who speak of a humanity cemented and armoured no longer with brutality but with love. They are welcome to deny that a maximum of physical power may coincide with a maximum of gentleness and goodness. Their critical scepticism cannot prevent the theory and experience of spiritual energy from combining to warn us that *we have reached a decisive point in human evolution*, at which the only way forward is in the direction

of a common passion, a 'conspira-
tion'.

To go on putting our hopes in a
social order obtained by external
violence would simply mean to
abandon all hope of carrying the
spirit of earth to its limits.

Now human energy, being the expression of a movement as irresistible
and infallible as the universe itself,
cannot possibly be prevented by any
obstacle from freely reaching the
natural goal of its evolution.

Therefore, despite all checks and
all improbabilities, we are inevitably
approaching a new age, in which the
world will throw off its chains and at
last give itself up to the power of its
inner affinities.

Either we must doubt the value of

everything around us, or we must utterly believe in the possibility, and I should now add, in the inevitable consequences, of universal love.

What are these consequences?

So far, in our study of the socio-totalizing love of human energy, we have principally considered its singular property of joining and articulating the thinking molecules of the noosphere without turning them into machines. But this is only the negative face of the phenomenon. Love has not only the virtue of uniting without depersonalizing, but in uniting it ultra-personalizes. From this pass that we have reached, what horizons appear before us in the skies of humanity?

Here, we must first of all look

backwards, to the point where we left the individual human nucleus, at the completion of its transformation by love. Under Omega's influence, we said, each separate soul becomes capable of breathing itself out in a single act into which the incalculable plurality of its perceptions and activities, its sufferings and desires, passes without confusion. Well, the sum of elementary energies constituting the global mass of human energy seems to be moving towards an analogous metamorphosis of a far higher order. We have followed, in the individual, the gradual assumption of the emotions, aspirations and actions in an indefinable operation *sui generis*, which is all these things at once and something more as well. The same phenomenon, on an incomparably greater scale, tends to take place under the same Omega influence in terrestrial thought collected as a whole. And indeed when the whole of humanity, operating and experiencing at the same time with its exploratory surface, the centre towards which it is converging; when the same fluid passion suffuses and connects the free diversity of attitudes, points of view and efforts, each represented in the universe by a particular unit of the human myriad; when the overflowing multitude of individual contradictions harmonizes in the profound simplicity of a single desire, what is all this but the genesis of a *collective and unique action*, in which, in

75

the sole conceivable form of love, the powers of personality comprised in the noosphere are realizing themselves, as they approach maturity, that is to say their final confluence?

Totalization of total human energy in a total love.

The ideal glimpsed in their dreams by the world technicians.

This, psychologically, is what love can do if carried to a universal degree.

But is this miracle *really* moving towards realization?

If it is, some traces of this prodigious transformation must be perceptible in history. Can we recognize them? This is what I have still to seek and show.

2. Love, the Historical Product of Human Evolution

The above analysis of the synthesizing power of love over the inner life was not made, and indeed could not be made, without some visible model.

Where then in nature today does a first sketch, a first approach to the total act of which we were apparently dreaming exist? Nowhere more clearly, I think, than in the act of Christian love as it can be performed by a modern believer for whom the creation has come to be expressed in terms of evolution. In such a man's eyes, the world's history bears the form of a vast cosmogenesis, in the course of which all the threads of reality converge without fusing in a Christ who is at the same time personal and universal. Strictly and unmetaphorically, the Christian who understands both the essence of his creed and nature's linkages in time and space, finds himself in the fortunate position of being, by all his various activities and in union with the crowd of his fellows, capable of surrendering to a unique act of communion. Whether he lives or dies, *by* his life and *by* his death, he in some sense completes his God, and is at the same time mastered by him. In short, comparable in every way to the Omega point which our theory led us to foresee, Christ (provided he reveals himself in the full realism of his incarnation) *tends to produce exactly the* spiritual totalization that we expected.

In itself the existence, even in detachment, of a state of consciousness endowed with such riches would bring, if fully established, a substantial verification of the views that we have set out on the ultimate nature of human energy. But it is possible to push the demonstration very much further by observing that the appearance in man of the love of God, understood in the fullness that we give it here, is not a simple sporadic accident, but appears as the regular product of a long evolution.

– from *Human Energy*, translated by J. M. Cohen, pp. 128-30, 144-55.

7

LOVE AS ENERGY

We are accustomed to consider (and with what a refinement of analysis!) only the sentimental face of love, the joy and miseries it causes us. It is in its natural dynamism and its evolutionary significance that I shall be dealing with it here, with a view to determining the ultimate phases of the phenomenon of man.

Considered in its full biological reality, love – that is to say, the affinity of being with being – is not peculiar to man. It is a general property of all life and as such it embraces, in its varieties and degrees, all the forms successively adopted by organized matter. In the mammals, so close to ourselves, it is easily recognized in its different modalities: sexual passion, parental instinct, social solidarity, etc. Farther off, that is to say lower down on the tree of life, analogies are more obscure until they become so faint as to be imperceptible. But this is the place to repeat what I said earlier when we were discussing the '*within* of things'. If there were no real internal propensity to unite, even at a prodigiously rudimentary level – indeed in the molecule itself – it would be physically impossible for love to appear higher up, with us, in 'hominized' form.

By rights, to be certain of its presence in ourselves, we should assume its presence, at least in an inchoate form, in everything that is. And in fact if we look around us at the confluent ascent of consciousness, we see it is not lacking anywhere. Plato felt this and has immortalized the idea in his *Dialogues*. Later, with thinkers like Nicolas of Cusa, medieval philosophy returned technically to the same notion. Driven by the forces of love, the fragments of the world seek each other so that the world may come to being. This is no metaphor; and it is much more than poetry. Whether as a force or a curvature, the universal gravity of bodies, so striking to us, is merely the reverse or shadow of that which really moves nature. To perceive cosmic energy 'at the fount' we must, if there is a *within* of things, go down into the internal or radial zone of spiritual attractions.

Love in all its subtleties is nothing more, and nothing less, than the more or less direct trace marked on the heart of the element by the psychical convergence of the universe upon itself.

This, if I am not mistaken, is the ray of light which will help us to see more clearly around us.

We are distressed and pained when we see modern attempts at human collectivization ending up, contrary to our expectations and theoretical predictions, in a lowering and an enslavement of consciousnesses. But so far how have we gone about the business of unification? A material situation to be defended; a new industrial field to be opened up, better conditions for a social class or less favoured nations – those are the only and very mediocre grounds on which we have so far tried to get together. There is no cause to be surprised if, in the footsteps of animal societies, we become mechanized in the very play of association. Even in the supremely intellectual activity of science (at any rate as long as it remains purely speculative and abstract) the impact of our souls only operates obliquely and indirectly. Contact is still superficial, involving the danger of yet another servitude. Love alone is capable of uniting living beings in such a way as to complete and fulfil them, for it alone takes them and joins them by what is deepest in themselves. This is a fact of daily experience. At what moment do lovers come into the most complete possession of themselves if not when they say they are lost in each other? In truth, does not love every instant achieve all around us, in the couple or the team, the magic feat, the feat reputed to be contradictory, of 'personalizing' by totalizing? And if that is what it can achieve daily on a small scale, why should it not repeat this one day on world-wide dimensions?

Mankind, the spirit of the earth, the synthesis of individuals and peoples, the paradoxical conciliation of the element with the whole, and of unity with multitude – all these are called Utopian and yet they are biologically necessary. And for them to be incarnated in the world all we may well need is to imagine our power of loving developing until it embraces the total of men and of the earth.

It may be said that this is the precise point at which we are invoking the impossible. Man's capacity, it may seem, is confined to giving his affection to one human being or to very few. Beyond that radius the heart does not carry, and there is only room for cold justice and cold reason. To love all and everyone is a contradictory and false gesture which only leads in the end to loving no one.

To that I would answer that if, as you claim, a universal love is impossible, how can we account for that irresistible instinct in our hearts which leads us towards unity whenever and in whatever direction our passions are stirred? A sense of the universe, a sense of the *all*, the nostalgia which seizes us when confronted by nature, beauty, music – these seem to be an expectation and awareness of a Great Presence. The 'mystics' and their commentators apart, how has psychology been able so consistently to ignore this fundamental vibration whose ring can be heard by every practised ear at the basis, or rather at the summit, of every great emotion? Resonance to the All – the keynote of pure poetry and pure religion. Once again: what does this phenomenon, which is born with thought and grows with it, reveal if not a deep accord between two realities which seek each other; the severed particle which trembles at the approach of 'the rest'?

We are often inclined to think that we have exhausted the various natural forms of love with a man's love for his wife, his children, his friends and to a certain extent for his country. Yet precisely the most fundamental form of passion is missing from this list, the one which, under the pressure of an involuting universe, precipitates the elements

one upon the other in the Whole –
cosmic affinity and hence cosmic
sense. A universal love is not only
psychologically possible; it is the
only complete and final way in which
we are able to love.

But, with this point made, how are
we to explain the appearance all
around us of mounting repulsion
and hatred? If such a strong potentiality is besieging us from within and
urging us to union, what is it waiting
for to pass from potentiality to action? Just this, no doubt: that we
should overcome the 'anti-person-
alist' complex which paralyses us,
and make up our minds to accept
the possibility, indeed the reality, of
some *source* of love and *object* of love
at the summit of the world above

our heads. So long as it absorbs or appears to absorb the person, collectivity kills the love that is trying to come to birth. As such collectivity is essentially unlovable. That is where philanthropic systems break down. Common sense is right. It is impossible to give oneself to an anonymous number. But if the universe ahead of us assumes a face and a heart, and so to speak personifies itself, then in the atmosphere created by this focus the elemental attraction will immediately blossom. Then, no doubt, under the heightened pressure of an infolding world, the formidable energies of attraction, still dormant between human molecules, will burst forth.

The discoveries of the last hundred

years, with their unitary perspectives, have brought a new and decisive impetus to our sense of the world, to our sense of the earth, and to our human sense. Hence the rise of modern pantheism. But this impetus will only end by plunging us back into super-matter unless it leads us towards someone.

For the failure that threatens us to be turned into success, for the concurrence of human monads to come about, it is necessary and sufficient for us that we should extend our science to its farthest limits and recognize and accept (as being necessary to close and balance space-time) not only some vague future existence, but also, as I must now stress, the radiation *as a present reality* of that mysterious centre of our centres which I have called Omega.

– from *The Phenomenon of Man*, translated by Bernard Wall, pp. 264-8.